Happy Birthday
COLORING BOOK

THIS BOOK BELONGS TO:

I GAVE BIRTH
28 YEARS AGO
WHERE'S MY CAKE?

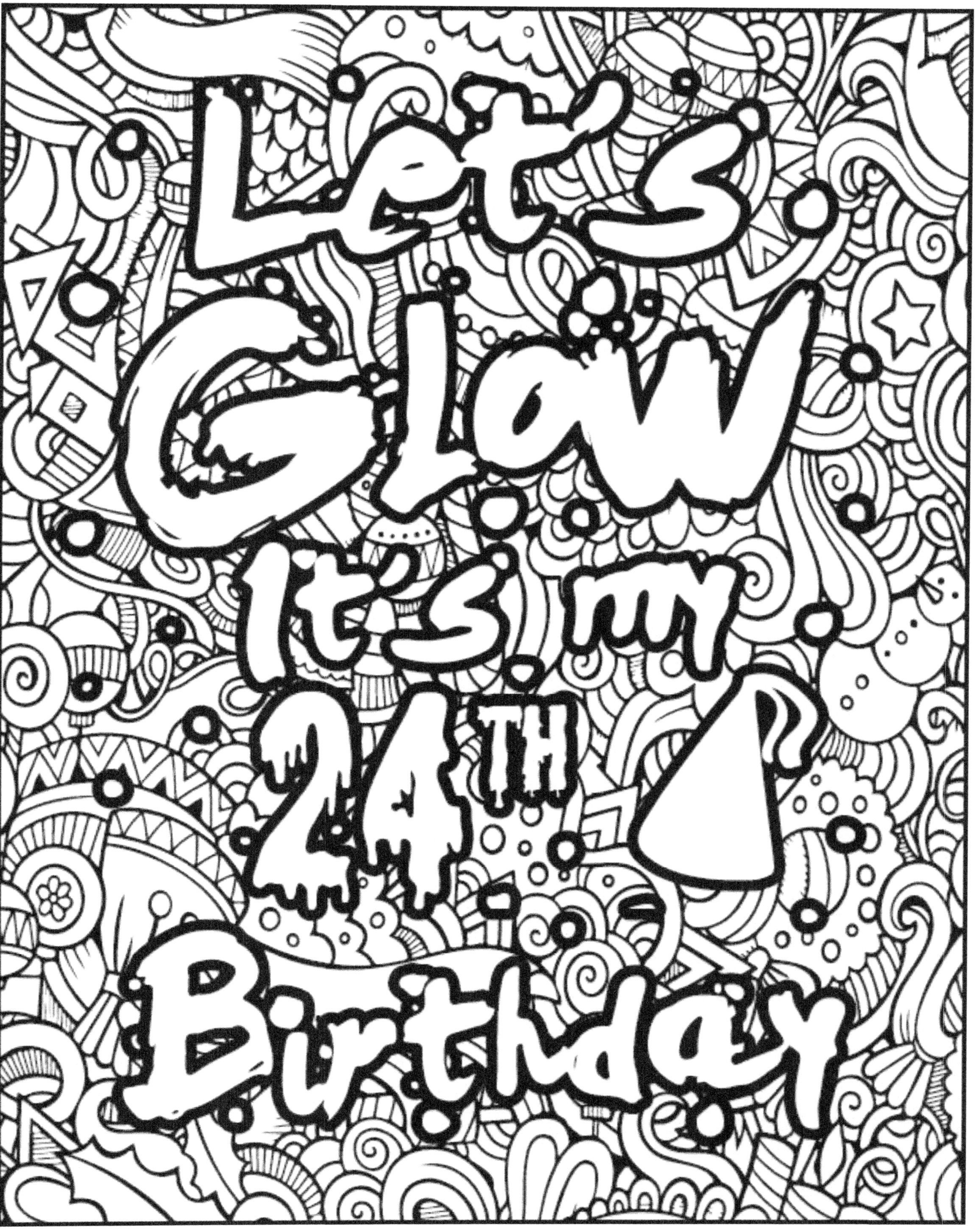
Let's
Glow
It's my
24TH
Birthday

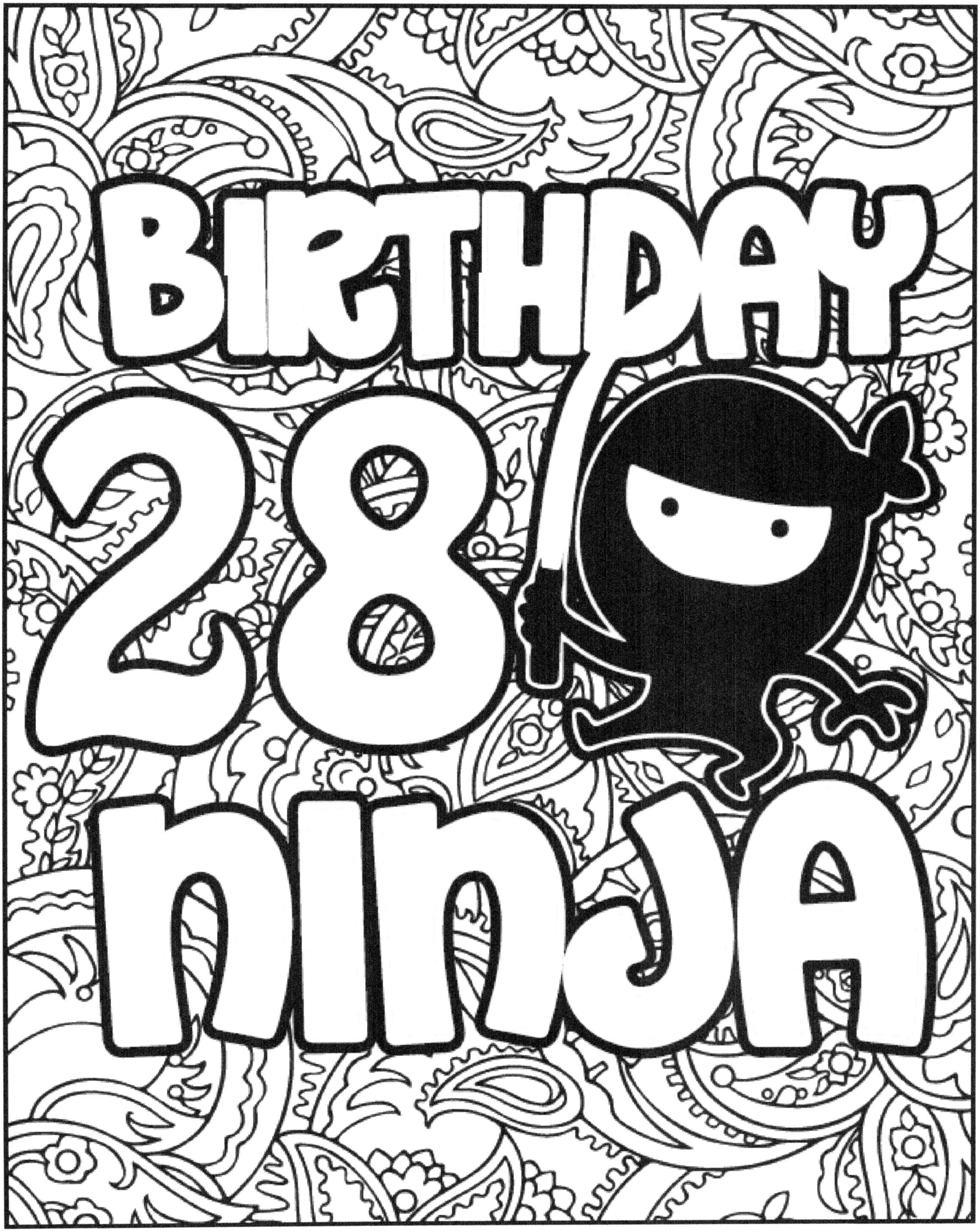
BIRTHDAY
28
NINJA

28
Birthday
QUEEN

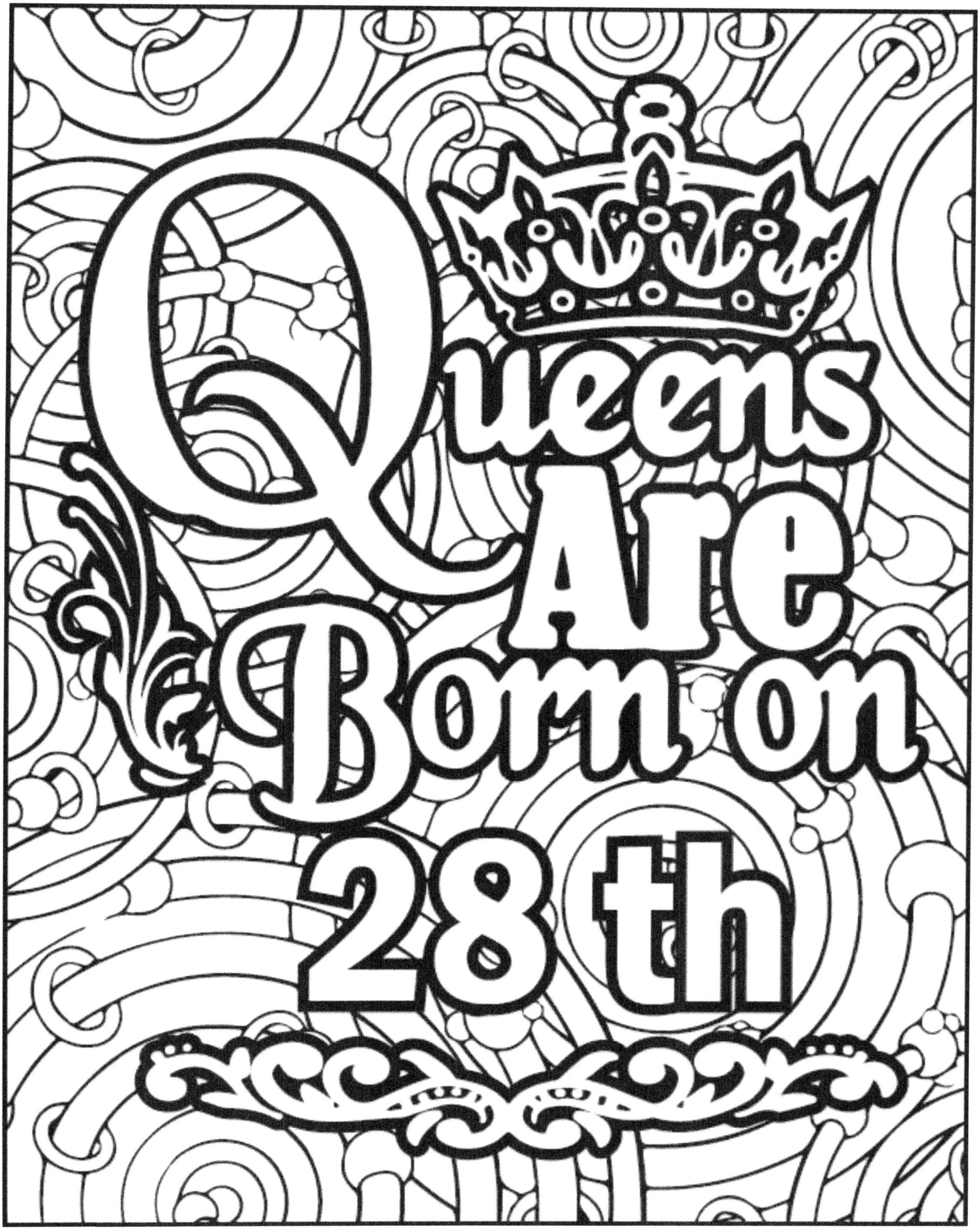
Queens
Are
Born on
28 th

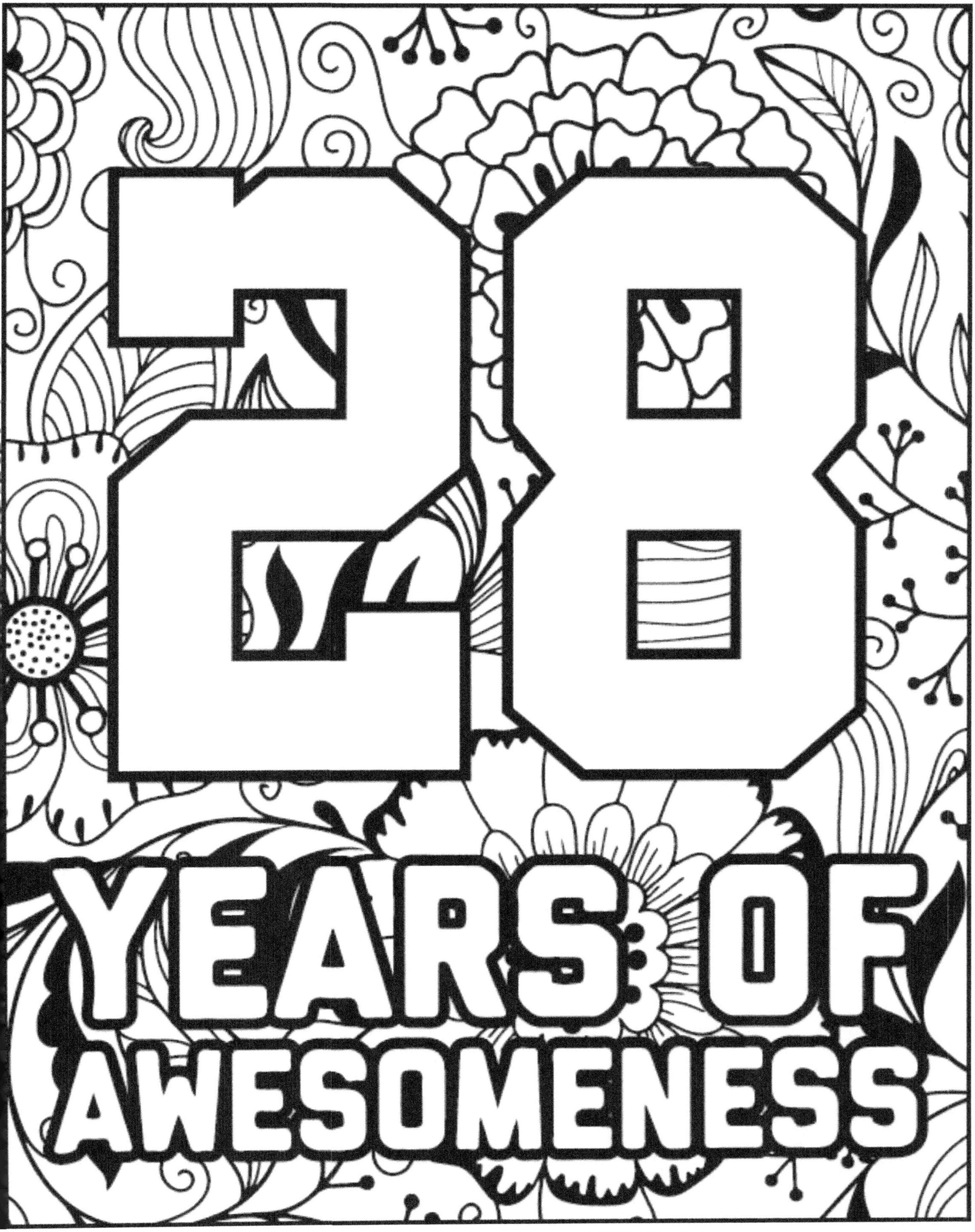
28
YEARS OF
AWESOMENESS

28
&
Fabulous

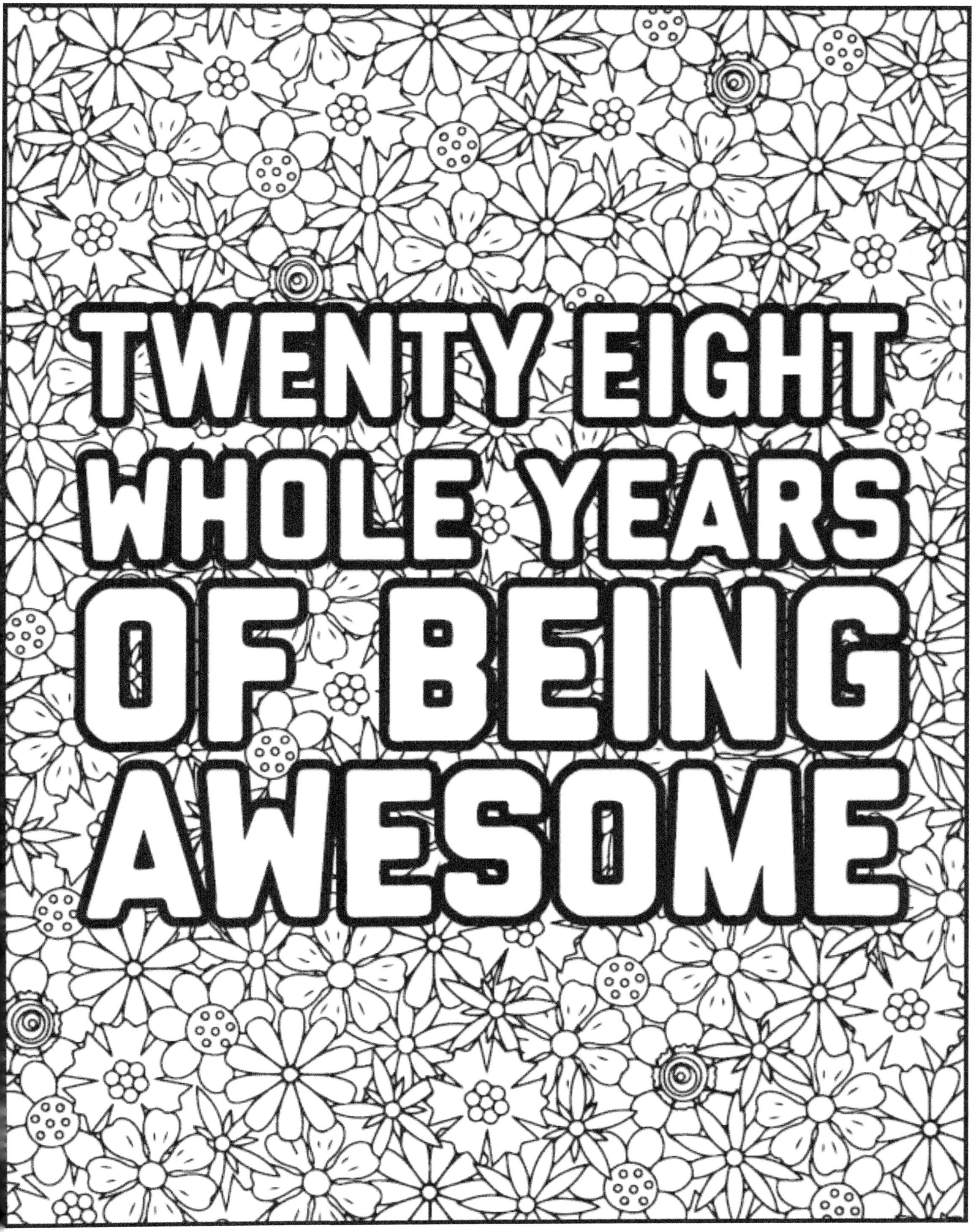
TWENTY EIGHT
WHOLE YEARS
OF BEING
AWESOME

LEVEL 28
COMPLETE

IT'S MY
Birthday
28

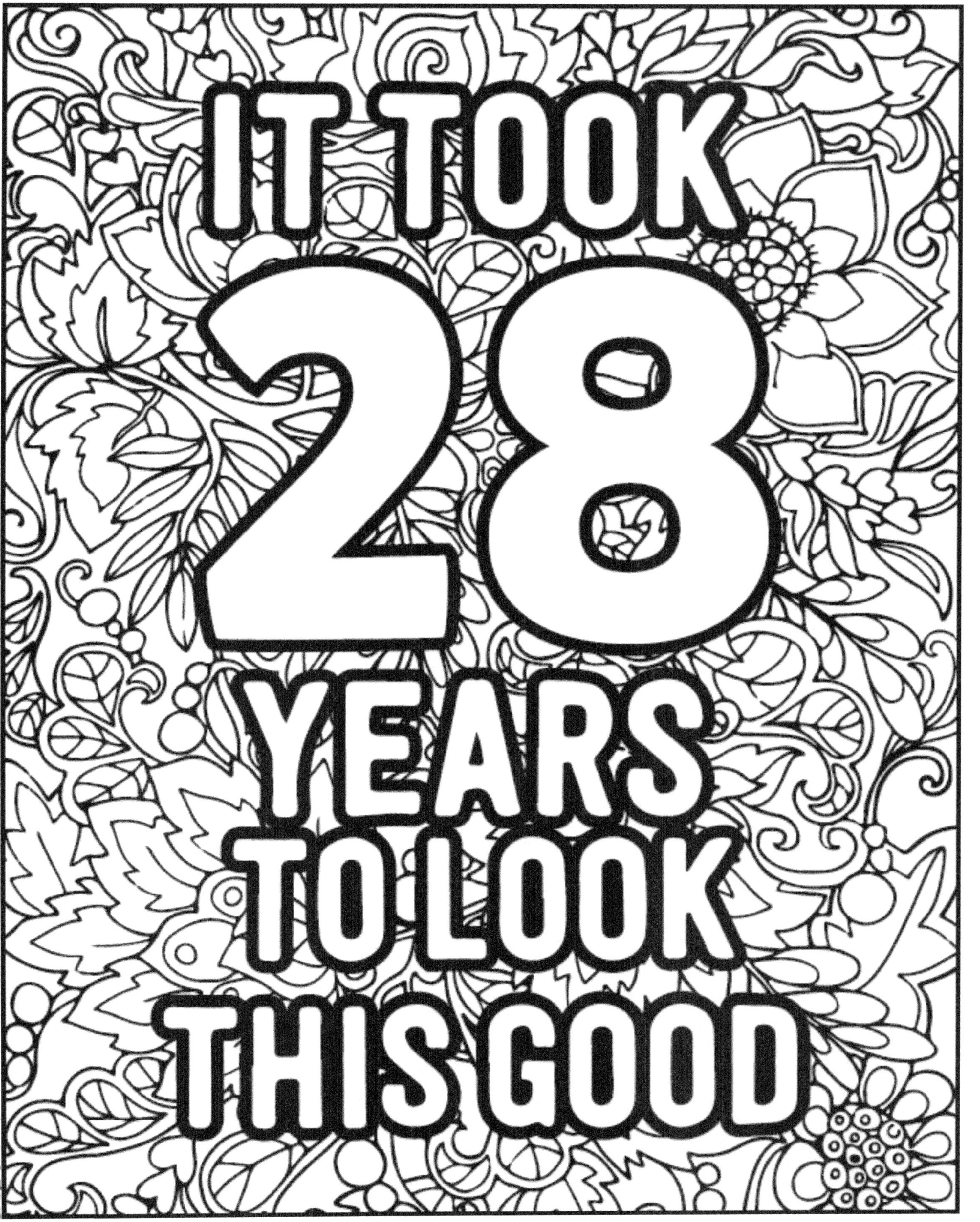
IT TOOK
28
YEARS
TO LOOK
THIS GOOD

I'M 28
Bitches

GOLDEN
28
BIRTHDAY

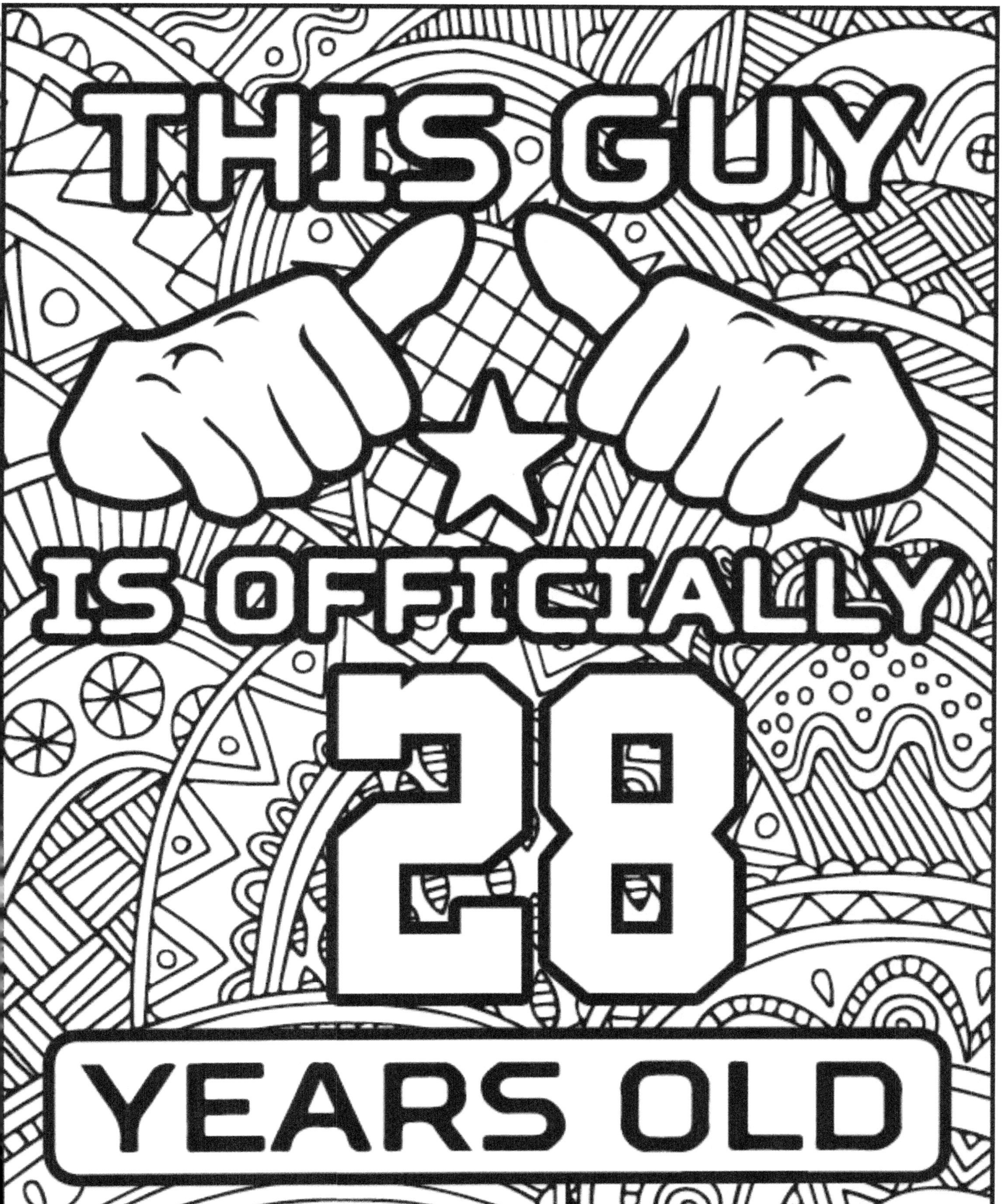
THIS GUY
IS OFFICIALLY
28
YEARS OLD

THIS IS WHAT AN
AWESOME
28
YEAR OLD
PRINCESS
LOOKS LIKE

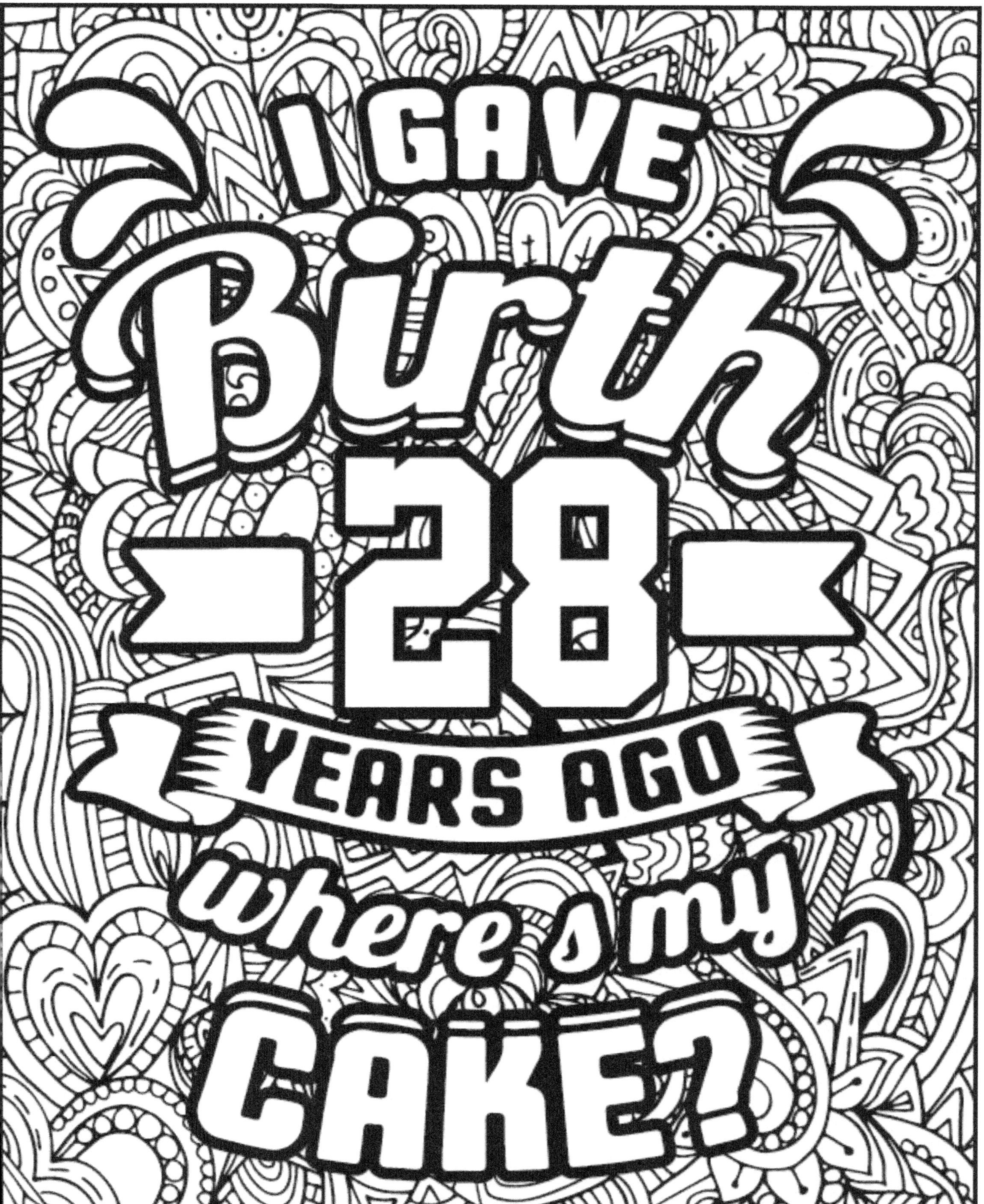
I GAVE
Birth
28
YEARS AGO
where's my
CAKE?

It's My
28th
Birthday

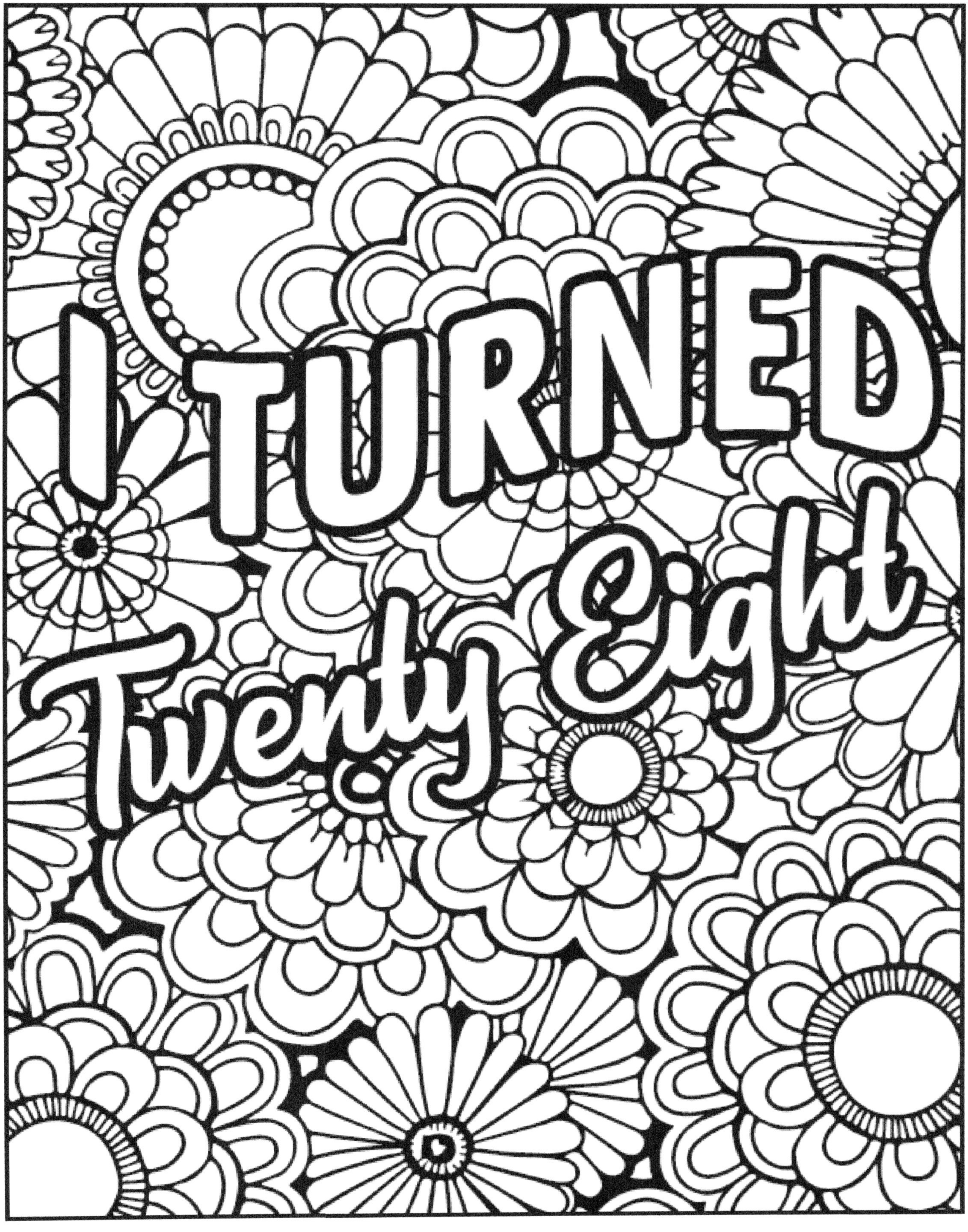
I TURNED
Twenty Eight

LEVEL 28
COMPLETE

28
BIRTHDAY
PRINCESS

28
KEEP
CALM
AND
PARTY
ON

Chapter
28

It's official...
28
I'm an adult!

28

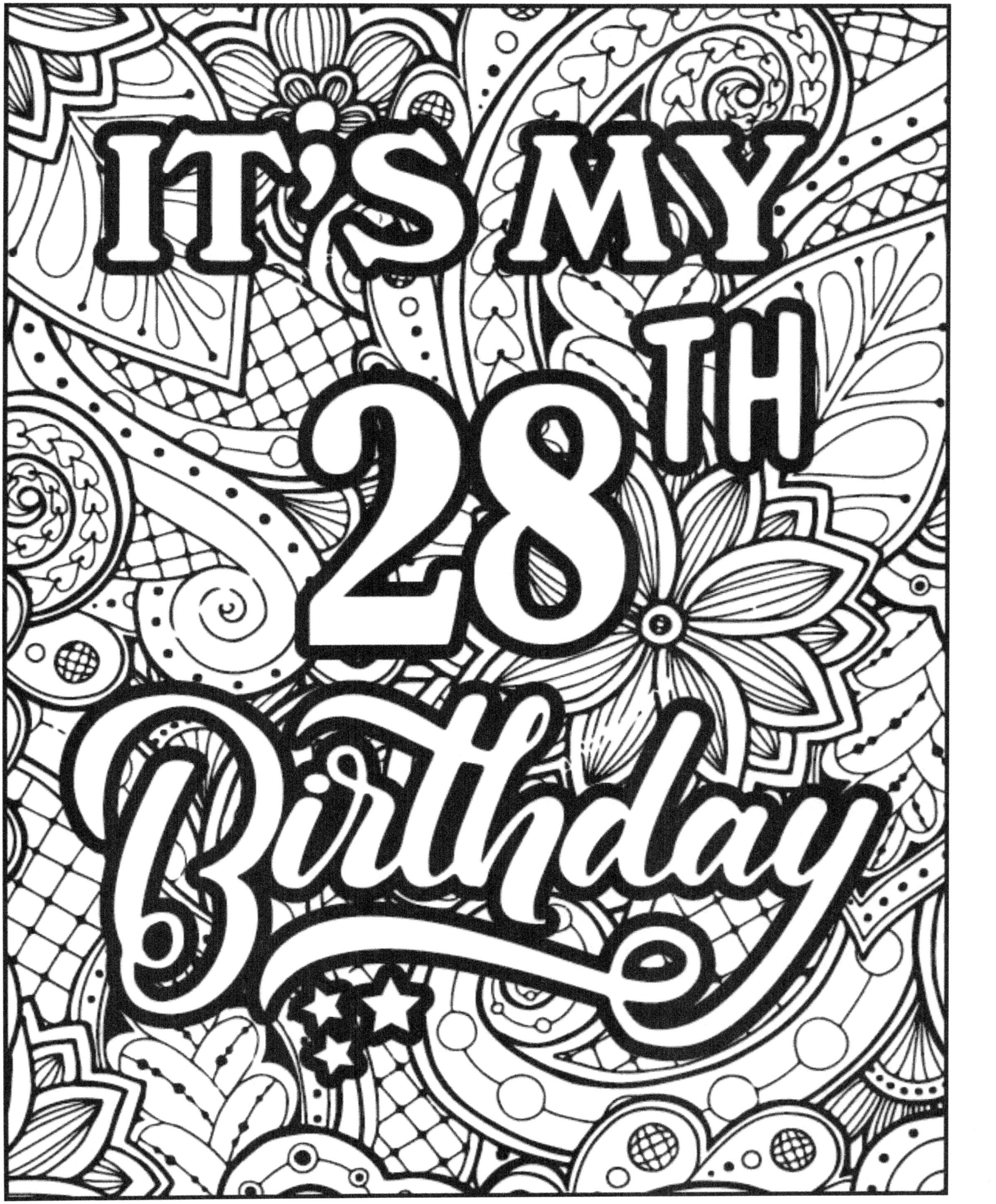
IT'S MY
28TH
Birthday

birthday
queen
28

LEVEL
28
UNLOCKED

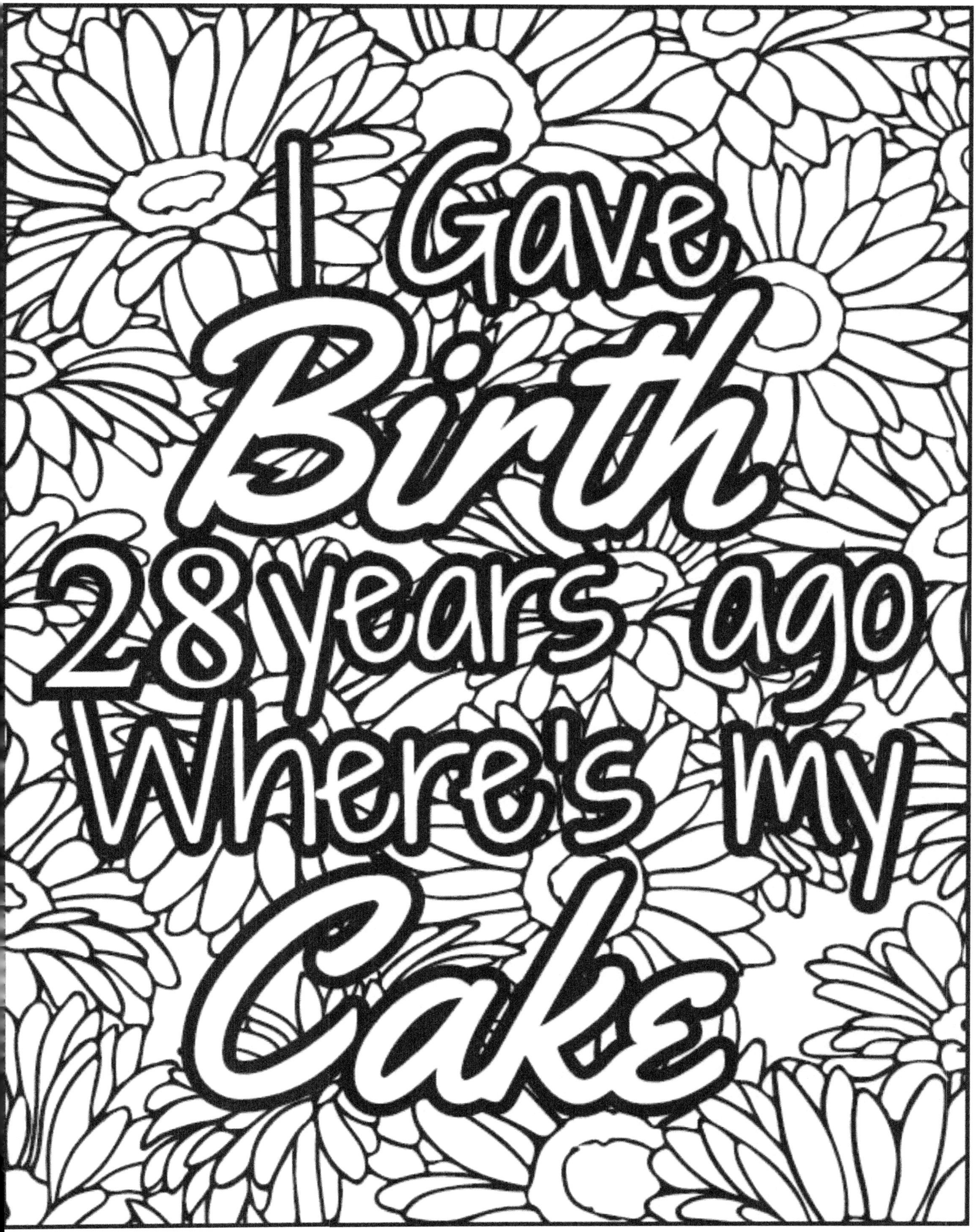
I Gave
Birth
28 years ago
Where's my
Cake

COLOR TEST

Printed in Great Britain
by Amazon

47258643R00037